MORE THAN A GAME

PATIENCE
AT THE PLATE

AND OTHER
BASEBALL SKILLS

by Elliott Smith

CAPSTONE PRESS
a capstone imprint

Published by Capstone Press, an imprint of Capstone.
1710 Roe Crest Drive
North Mankato, Minnesota 56003
capstonepub.com

Library of Congress Cataloging-in-Publication Data
Names: Smith, Elliott, 1976- author.
Title: Patience at the plate : and other baseball skills / Elliott Smith.
Description: North Mankato, Minnesota : Capstone Press, an imprint of Capstone, [2022] | Series: Sports illustrated kids: more than a game |Includes bibliographical references and index. | Audience: Ages 8-11 |Audience: Grades 4-6 | Summary: "There's more to being a great athlete than just winning the game. Today's baseball superstars know it takes talent, skill, and respect to make them great at the plate. This Sports Illustrated Kids title combines fast-paced action, famous plays, and SEL skills to show what sets your favorite athletes and teams apart-on and off the baseball diamond"-- Provided by publisher.
Identifiers: LCCN 2021008495 (print) | LCCN 2021008496 (ebook) | ISBN 9781663906670 (hardcover) | ISBN 9781663920591 (paperback) | ISBN 9781663906649 (pdf) | ISBN 9781663906663 (kindle edition)
Subjects: LCSH: Baseball--Juvenile literature.
Classification: LCC GV867.5 .S59 2021 (print) | LCC GV867.5 (ebook) | DDC 796.357--dc23
LC record available at https://lccn.loc.gov/2021008495
LC ebook record available at https://lccn.loc.gov/2021008496

Image Credits
Associated Press: David J. Philip, 21, Eric Risberg, 24, 29, Jeff Chiu, 18, Jose Luis Magana, File, 13, Marcio Jose Sanchez, 22, Matt York, 19; Getty Images: JohnnyGreig, 5; iStockphoto: PeopleImages, Cover, (right middle); Newscom: Icon Sportswire 749/Mark Goldman, 17, Image of Sport, 15, UPI/Kamil Krzaczynski, 25; Shutterstock: Avector, (dots) design element, Dan Thornberg (baseball) design element, Eugene Onischenko, (arena) design element; Fuller Photography, Cover, (right top), Gertan, 4, sirtravelalot, Cover, (right bottom); Sports Illustrated: Erick W. Rasco/Contributor, 6, 7, 9, 10, 12, 27, 28

Editorial Credits
Editor: Alison Deering; Designer: Heidi Thompson; Media Researcher: Morgan Walters; Production Specialist: Tori Abraham

TABLE OF CONTENTS

Glossary terms are **BOLD** on first use.

DIAMOND DREAMS

Baseball is a game of many challenges. Athletes use their strength, speed, and coordination in order to succeed.

Baseball is also a great way to learn social and emotional skills. Players must work together and combine their talents to become a good team. They learn to how to set goals and work to achieve them. This is true at all levels, from T-ball to Little League to Major League Baseball (MLB).

Athletes also use their curiosity to study and gain new talents. That might mean adjusting their batting **stance** or trying out a different pitch. It's about putting in the work to find what works.

The sport can be hard. The best players, coaches, and teams prove patience, **motivation,** and problem-solving can lead to success on the baseball diamond.

PATIENCE

Even the best hitters in baseball make an out seven out of 10 times. That's why patience is key in this sport. Hitting a home run or striking out the side—striking out all three batters in an inning—doesn't happen all the time. Patient players know how to put themselves in a position to succeed.

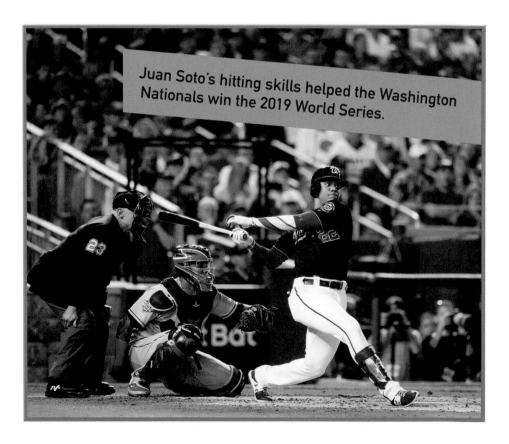

Juan Soto's hitting skills helped the Washington Nationals win the 2019 World Series.

Star in the Making

Juan Soto of the Washington Nationals is one of the youngest players in MLB. But since making his MLB debut at age 19 in 2018, Soto has shown patience beyond his years. He is one of the most selective batters in baseball.

Soto aims to only swing at pitches he likes. After his third season, Soto already has 228 career walks. When pitchers try to get him to chase poor throws, Soto's bat doesn't move. But when they make mistakes, Soto hits the ball hard.

Soto led the National League in batting average in 2020, hitting .351. His patience at the plate means he is one of baseball's most feared hitters.

"I've been really proud about being patient and taking my walks," Soto said.

Soto is known for taking his time at the plate and waiting for the right pitch.

World Series Marathon

Each pitch of the World Series is important. But in Game 3 of the 2018 World Series, that was taken to the next level. The Boston Red Sox and Los Angeles Dodgers squared off in a game that turned into a test of patience.

The teams were tied 1–1 after nine innings. In the thirteenth inning, it looked as if the Red Sox had broken through, scoring a run. The Dodgers, however, tied it again. The game marched on . . . and on.

The pressure built with each inning. Both teams needed to stay focused, even when tired. It took concentration, patience, and strength to keep going.

It took until the eighteenth inning for a victor to emerge. Max Muncy hit a **walk-off home run** for the Dodgers, winning the game 3–2. The longest game in World Series history lasted 7 hours and 20 minutes.

The first World Series was played in 1903 between the Pittsburgh Pirates and the Boston Americans, now known as the Boston Red Sox. Boston won, 5 games to 3, in the best-of-nine series.

Fans watch as Max Muncy gets ready to hit what would be the game-winning home run.

MVP Mike

Mike Trout of the Los Angeles Angels sets the standard for being a calm and smart player. The three-time Most Valuable Player (MVP) uses a patient approach at the plate. It has resulted in huge numbers for one of the top players in the game.

Over the course of his 10-year career, Trout has hit 302 home runs. He also led the league in on-base percentage for four straight seasons. For three of those four seasons, Trout led both the American League and the National League combined.

Trout could simply use his natural ability to make most plays. Instead, he does his homework to get even better. The center fielder studies opposing hitters and uses his speed and footwork to make amazing catches. The hard work has paid off. Trout is one of baseball's best defensive players.

MLB is divided into two leagues. The National League formed in 1876, and the American League was created in 1901. American League teams play with a "designated hitter." This player doesn't play the field and bats in place of the pitcher. In the National League, the pitcher bats along with the other players.

PROBLEM-SOLVING

There are times where baseball players, coaches, and staff run into issues. It might be injury related. It might be how to best maximize talent. Or it could be figuring out which players work best together to create a successful team. Either way, if something isn't working, you have to fix it. That is why problem-solving is a key aspect of the sport.

Pitcher Stephen Strasburg had to figure out a way to protect his throwing arm from injury.

Strasburg (center) helped his team win the 2019 World Series.

It's a Stretch

After suffering a series of injuries, Washington Nationals Stephen Strasburg decided a change was in order. He may have been an All-Star pitcher, but it was at the cost of getting hurt every season.

Strasburg used problem-solving to help his career. For seven years he pitched one way. Then, he decided to tweak his pitching motion. Instead of throwing from a full windup, like most pitchers, Strasburg only threw from the stretch position. This is the position pitchers use when there is a runner on base.

Strasburg's **perseverance** and creativity paid off. The change helped relieve pressure on his repaired elbow. He won 18 games in 2019 and was named MVP of the World Series.

Blazing a New Trail

Building a team is a complex puzzle. Much of putting the puzzle together falls to a team's general manager. The general manager makes the decisions about which players and coaches are on the squad. It requires knowledge of the game and knowing how all the players fit together.

For Kim Ng, the general manager of the Miami Marlins, it's a challenge she welcomes. For years, Ng has stayed determined in the face of rejection. After being turned down for similar jobs by at least five teams, Ng made history in November 2020 when she became the first female general manager in baseball history.

Ng has a long, 30-year career working in the sport and is excited about building the Marlins. She knows that many people will look to her for inspiration in her new role.

"People are looking for hope. People are looking for inspiration. I'm happy that this is a part of it," Ng said.

Before Kim Ng, a woman has never been a general manager in the MLB.

A Different Thinker

Trevor Bauer is curious and a problem-solver. As a pitcher, he likes to try new things when it comes to his work. He'll do whatever it takes to solve a problem and become a better pitcher. He uses computer technology to study the **spin rate** of his pitches. A long, wobbly shoulder tube helps loosen up Bauer's arm. And he takes part in extreme sessions of long toss before a game. While most pitchers usually throw about 60 feet in these sessions, Bauer tries to throw 300 feet.

None of Bauer's methods are common. But the results work well for him. In 2020, as a member of the Cincinnati Reds, he won the National League Cy Young Award for best pitcher with a career-low 1.73 earned run average (ERA). In 2021, Bauer signed with the Los Angeles Dodgers and became the highest-paid MLB player for the next two seasons, earning $40 million in 2021 and $45 million in 2022.

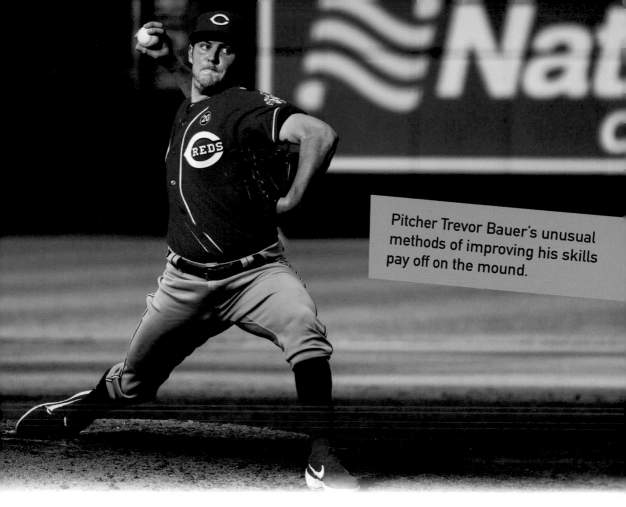

Pitcher Trevor Bauer's unusual methods of improving his skills pay off on the mound.

Launch It!

Justin Turner was almost at the end of his career. After struggling with the New York Mets, the third baseman signed with the Los Angeles Dodgers. It was likely his last shot. So he decided to change his swing.

Turner focused more on launch angle—swinging the bat upward so the ball went in the air more. Quickly, Turner found his power stroke. He hit 27 homers in 2016 and again in 2019. He blasted more than 30 doubles three seasons in a row. Turner became one of the leaders of the swing revolution that has changed baseball.

TEAMWORK

Baseball is not an individual game. From players to coaches, everyone must work together to ensure victory. Teammates need to practice together to learn each other's strengths and weaknesses. Friendship and connection go a long way in creating a great team.

Coaching Dreams

After Alyssa Nakken finished her college softball career at Sacramento State, she thought her athletic days were over. A few years later, she landed an **internship** with the San Francisco Giants. She was working for the team when Gabe Kapler interviewed to be their manager.

Alyssa Nakken on the field as first base coach for the San Francisco Giants

Nakken coaching during a Giants batting practice in 2020

When Kapler was hired, he reached out to Nakken. She was one of the people he had spoken to when he interviewed, and Kapler wanted to add her to his staff.

Nakken made history when she became MLB's first full-time female coach. She works closely with other coaches and players, teaching outfield positioning, base-stealing technique, and other performance skills.

Nakken's drive and determination have paid off. In July 2020, she made history again when she coached first base during an **exhibition** game.

A Team Comeback

When things go bad, it can be easy to give up. But the Washington Nationals didn't believe that. In 2019, their teamwork helped take them from a 19–31 record all the way to the World Series.

That team-first attitude helped them again in Game 7 of that World Series. The Nationals trailed the Houston Astros 2–0 going into the seventh inning. But several players stepped up with big efforts. **Veteran** Howie Kendrick hit a go-ahead home run off the screen attached to the foul pole. Patrick Corbin came out of the bullpen to pitch several key innings. And **closer** Daniel Hudson helped finish the game, making the Nationals champions in a remarkable 6–2 victory.

"I believe in these guys," Nationals manager Dave Martinez said. "They believe in each other. And the biggest thing for us is, never quit."

The Washington Nationals celebrated on the field after winning the 2019 World Series.

Shortstop Fernando Tatis Jr. throws the ball while Manny Machado watches.

Dynamic Duo

The left side of the infield is a key defensive area for baseball teams. The third baseman and shortstop must work together to stop hard-hit balls. No team in baseball has a better defensive duo than Manny Machado and Fernando Tatis Jr. of the San Diego Padres.

Machado is a veteran at third base. Tatis, a young player, is at shortstop. The two are among the best in the league at their positions. Machado has twice won a Gold Glove, given to the best defensive player at every position. Tatis figures to win one soon.

Together, Machado and Tatis are even stronger. In the 2020 season, the pair helped the Padres make the playoffs for the first time since 2006. Together they showed that hard work and determination can add up to victory.

"We push each other," Machado said of Tatis. "It's good to have him on our side and next to me every single day, because every single player needs that. We need people to push us to be the best we possibly can."

MOTIVATION AND PERSEVERANCE

Baseball players at all levels set goals to motivate themselves. Whether its striking out five batters in a Little League game or hitting .300 in MLB, working hard to achieve goals is important. Sometimes, reaching those goals can be hard. Perseverance is key when players need to push through the tough times before triumph.

Shortstop Tim Anderson throws to first during a 2020 game against the Oakland Athletics.

Hitting Machine

Tim Anderson believes in himself. The Chicago White Sox shortstop set a goal to become one of baseball's best players. He is delivering on his promise. Anderson has developed into a strong hitter for his team. In 2019, Anderson led the majors in batting average, hitting .335.

As one of the game's most prominent Black players, Anderson wants to help change the face of baseball. Over the years, the number of Black players in MLB has declined. In 2020, fewer than eight percent were Black.

Anderson uses those numbers as motivation. His goal is to bring back fun to the game. So flashy plays and bat flips are part of his game. But he backs up his bravado. In 2020, Anderson earned the Silver Slugger Award after hitting .322.

Anderson's persistence at the plate has paid off.

The Judge is In

It's hard to imagine Aaron Judge ever struggling. But the New York Yankees slugger didn't always hit the cover off the ball.

When he first arrived in New York, Judge had trouble handling MLB pitching. He hit .179 with 42 strikeouts in 2016, his rookie season. But Judge persevered. He was motivated to do better. He spent the offseason working to improve his swing. He studied video of his at-bats to fix flaws at the plate.

Since 2016, Judge has become one of the best power hitters in baseball. He hit 52 homers the very next season. He keeps his .179 batting average written at the top of the notes app on his phone so he doesn't forget the struggles he overcame.

"It's motivation to tell you don't take anything for granted," Judge said. "This game will humble you in a heartbeat."

Aaron Judge has persisted as a hitter in the MLB by constantly working to improve his swing.

Long Road Back

Daniel Bard was a relief pitcher in 2011. But just as quick as one of his fastballs, he lost the ability to throw strikes. He had, what is known in baseball terms, as "the yips."

His teammates supported Bard. Following a game, Bard found a note in his locker, which read, "You don't know how much respect we all have for what you're continuing to battle through."

Bard was out of baseball for seven years. But the desire to pitch never left. And in 2020, having overcome the yips, Bard returned with the Colorado Rockies. He finished with a 4–2 record, six saves, and the Comeback Player of the Year award.

Tough Cookie

At the start of the 2019 season, Carlos Carrasco was one of the top pitchers in baseball. The Cleveland Indians star was firing on all cylinders. But in the summer of 2019, Carrasco faced a major setback. He found out he had **leukemia**.

Pitcher Carlos Carrasco did not let cancer end his outstanding pitching career.

Carrasco, nicknamed Cookie for his favorite snack, fought hard against the disease. Just three months later, Carrasco returned to the game. In September 2019, he pitched an inning of relief and was later named the 2019 Comeback Player of the Year.

In July 2020, Carrasco made his first start since getting healthy. He struck out 10 players in six innings, earning a very emotional victory in his triumph over cancer. In 2021, he moved to the New York Mets, following a trade.

"I went through a lot," Carrasco said. "But for me, I never put anything really bad in my mind. It's always something good. And that's what I did from Day 1 until now."

Carrasco (right) shakes the hand of a coach in 2019.

GLOSSARY

closer (KLOH-zer)—a pitcher brought in during the late innings, usually to save the game

exhibition (ek-suh-BI-shuhn)—a preseason game played only for show that does not count toward team or player rankings

humble (HUHM-buhl)—to easily and unexpectedly defeat

internship (in-TURN-ship)—a temporary job in which a person works with and learns from experienced workers

leukemia (loo-KEE-mee-uh)—cancer that affects blood cells

motivation (moh-tuh-VEY-shuhn)—a force or influence that causes someone to do something

perseverance (pur-suh-VEER-uhns)—the quality that allows someone to continue trying to do something even though it is difficult

spin rate (SPIN RAYT)—the amount of spin on a baseball after it is released; the higher the spin, the more change in movement

stance (STANS)—the position of a batter's feet and body

veteran (VETer-uhn)—a person who has a lot of experience at a particular job or activity

walk-off home run (WALK-off HOME RUN)—a game-winning home run in the bottom half of the last inning of a game

READ MORE

Burrell, Dean. *Baseball Biographies for Kids: The Greatest Players from the 1960s to Today*. Emeryville, CA: Rockridge Press, 2020.

Chandler, Matt. *Mike Trout: Baseball's MVP*. North Mankato, MN: Capstone Press, 2021.

MacKinnon, Adam C. *Baseball for Kids: A Young Fan's Guide to the History of the Game*. Emeryville, CA: Rockbridge Press, 2020.

INTERNET SITES

Little League
littleleague.org

MLB Play Ball
playball.org

Sports Illustrated Kids Baseball
sikids.com/baseball

INDEX